Deliciou
APPETIZERS
and SNACKS
WITH
HERBS

DAWN J. RANCK and
PHYLLIS PELLMAN GOOD

Good Books

Intercourse, PA 17534

Cover design and illustration by Cheryl Benner
Design by Dawn J. Ranck
Illustrations by Cheryl Benner

DELICIOUSLY EASY APPETIZERS AND SNACKS WITH HERBS
Copyright © 1998 by Good Books, Intercourse, Pennsylvania, 17534
International Standard Book Number: 1-56148-261-7
Library of Congress Catalog Card Number: 98-41851

Library of Congress Cataloging-in-Publication Data
Ranck, Dawn J.
    Deliciously easy appetizers and snacks with herbs / Dawn J.
Ranck and Phyllis Pellman Good.
        p. cm. -- (Deliciously easy -- with herbs)
        ISBN 1-56148-261-7
        1. Appetizers. 2. Snack foods. 3. Cookery (Herbs)
I. Good, Phyllis Pellman. II. Title. III. Series: Ranck, Dawn J.
Deliciously easy -- with herbs.
TX740.R34 1998
641.8'12--dc21   98-41851
                                                                    CIP

Table of Contents

Baked Herb Cheese Spread

Danielle Vachow
Busha's Brae Herb Farm
Suttons Bay, MI

Makes 24 small wedges

8-oz. pkg. cream cheese,
  softened
2 eggs, beaten
1/2 cup sour cream
1 tsp. Dijon mustard
1/4 cup chopped fresh herbs
  (5 tsp. dried): choose one,
  or any combination of, thyme,
  oregano, rosemary, dill,
  tarragon, basil, parsley

1 clove garlic, minced
1/4 tsp. coarsely ground
  pepper

1. Beat together cream cheese and eggs until smooth. Add sour cream and mustard.
2. Fold in herbs, garlic, and pepper.
3. Spread mixture into greased 2-2 1/2 cup mold or 2 8"-springform pans.
4. Bake at 350° for 30 minutes, or until center is firm.
5. Cool. Unmold onto serving dish. Cut each round into 12 pie-shaped wedges.
6. Garnish with fresh herbs or edible flowers. Serve with whole wheat or wafer crackers.

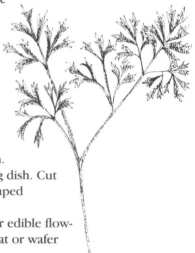

Herbal Cheese Spread

Lynn Redding
Redding's Country Cabin
Ronda, NC

Makes 20 servings

8-oz. pkg. cream cheese,
   softened
1/4 cup margarine, softened
11/2 Tbsp. milk
1/4 tsp. garlic powder
3/4 tsp. chopped fresh savory
   (1/4 tsp. dried)

1/2 tsp. chopped fresh
   oregano (1/8 tsp. dried)
1/2 tsp. chopped fresh dill
   (1/8 tsp. dried)
1/2 tsp. chopped fresh basil
   (1/8 tsp. dried)
1/8 tsp. black pepper

1. Beat together cream cheese and margarine until fluffy. Add milk and mix well.
2. Stir in seasonings and herbs. Mix well.
3. Serve with crackers or on hot vegetables or hot pasta.

Herbal Cream Cheese

Jacoba Baker & Reenie Baker Sandsted
Baker's Acres
Groton, NY

Makes 2 cups spread

2 8-oz. pkgs. cream cheese,
   softened
2 Tbsp. cream
1 Tbsp. fresh dill
   (1 tsp. dried)

2 tsp. fresh basil leaves
   (2/3 tsp. dried)
1-2 cloves garlic

1. Mix together all ingredients in food processor. Process until herbs and garlic are chopped.
2. Chill for 8 hours. Use with fresh vegetables or crackers.

Garden Party Herb Terrine

Nancy J. Reppert
Sweet Remembrances
Mechanicsburg, PA

Makes 20 servings

2 8-oz. pkgs. cream cheese, softened
1/2 cup crumbled feta cheese
1/2 tsp. garlic powder
1/4 tsp. ground red pepper
1/2 cup sour cream
2 eggs
2 1/2 tsp. shredded lemon peel
1/2 cup fresh garden herbs (any combination), chopped
1/4 cup thinly sliced green onion
1/2 cup chopped pimento
1/3 cup chopped black olives
1/2 cup chopped parsley
fresh edible flowers

1. Beat cream cheese until smooth. Add feta cheese, garlic powder, and red pepper. Beat well.
2. Stir in sour cream, eggs, and lemon peel. Beat just until blended.
3. Stir in 1/2 cup herbs, onion, pimento, and olives.
4. Pour into 8" x 4" loaf pan, with its sides greased and its bottom lined with foil.
5. Place loaf pan into large baking pan. Fill larger pan to a depth of 1" with boiling water.
6. Bake at 325° for 50 minutes, or until center is soft set. Remove from water bath and cool on wire rack for 1 hour. Cover and chill for at least 8 hours.
7. Gently remove from pan. Press chopped parsley around edges and garnish with edible flowers.
8. Serve with crackers.

Homestyle Boursin

Jacoba Baker & Reenie Baker Sandsted
Baker's Acres
Groton, NY

Makes 25-30 servings

2 8-oz. pkgs. cream cheese,
 softened
1/4 cup light mayonnaise
2 tsp. Dijon mustard
2 Tbsp. fresh chives,
 finely chopped (2 tsp. dried)

2 Tbsp. fresh dill,
 finely chopped
 (2 tsp. dried)
1 clove garlic, minced

1. Beat cheese, mayonnaise, and mustard until thoroughly blended.
2. Stir in chives, dill, and garlic. Mix well. Chill for 8 hours.
3. Serve as spread on crackers.

Fool's Boursin

Maryland Massey
Maryland's Herb Basket
Millington, MD

Makes 2 1/2 -3 cups

2 8-oz. pkgs. cream cheese,
 softened
8-oz. unsalted butter,
 softened
2 garlic cloves, minced
1 tsp. fresh marjoram
 (1/4 tsp. dried)
1 1/2 tsp. fresh dill
 (1/2 tsp. dried)

1 1/2 tsp. fresh basil
 (1/2 tsp. dried)
3/4 tsp. fresh thyme
 (1/4 tsp. dried)
1/4 tsp. pepper
1 tsp. Worcestershire sauce

1. Combine all ingredients.
2. Serve on crackers, toast, or muffins.

Note: Keeps for weeks in refrigerator.

Boursin-Style Cheese Spread

Mary Ellen Wilcox
South Ridge Treasures Herb Shop
Scotia, NY

Makes 1 1/2 cups

8-oz. pkg cream cheese, softened
1 stick unsalted butter, softened
1/4 tsp. red wine vinegar
1/2 tsp. Worcestershire sauce
1 clove garlic, minced
1 1/2 tsp. chopped fresh parsley (1/2 tsp. dried)
1 1/2 tsp. chopped fresh dill (1/2 tsp. dried)

3/4 tsp. chopped fresh basil (1/4 tsp. dried)
3/8 tsp. chopped fresh marjoram (1/8 tsp. dried)
3/8 tsp. chopped fresh thyme (1/8 tsp. dried)
1/4 tsp. chopped fresh rosemary (dash of dried)
dash of cayenne pepper

1. Combine cream cheese and butter. Mix well.
2. Stir in vinegar and Worcestershire sauce. Blend well.
3. Add garlic, herbs and cayenne. Blend well.
4. Refrigerate for several hours or overnight before serving.
5. Use as a spread for crackers, a topping for sandwiches, or spread for bagels.

Note: This will keep several weeks in the refrigerator.

Rosemary's Garlic Cheese Spread

Bertha Reppert
The Rosemary House
Mechanicsburg, PA

Makes 1 3/4 cups

8 oz. cream cheese, softened
1/2 cup butter, softened
1/2 tsp. Worcestershire sauce
1 clove garlic, minced
1 1/2 tsp. chopped fresh dill
   (1/2 tsp. dried)
1 1/2 tsp. chopped fresh basil
   (1/2 tsp. dried)

1 1/2 tsp. chopped fresh
   oregano (1/2 tsp. dried)
3/4 tsp. chopped fresh thyme
   (1/4 tsp. dried)
3/4 tsp. chopped fresh
   rosemary (1/4 tsp. dried)

1. Mix together all ingredients.
2. Spread on crackers, bagels, or sandwiches.

Variation: Eliminate butter; mix together all other ingredients.

Sweet Herbed Cheese

Bertha Reppert
The Rosemary House
Mechanicsburg, PA

Makes approximately 2 cups

8 oz. cream cheese, softened
8 oz. ricotta cheese
2 Tbsp. chopped orange zest
orange juice, enough to thin
   cheese to desired consistency
3 Tbsp. honey
1/4 cup coarsely chopped nuts

2 Tbsp. chopped peeled
   fresh ginger
4 Tbsp. chopped fresh herbs
   (rose geranium, mint,
   lemon verbena, rose
   petals, lemon balm, or a
   combination of any of
   those)

1. Combine all ingredients until smooth.
2. Serve with fresh fruit or vanilla wafers.

Veggie Dill Dip

Donna Treloar
Harmony
Gaston, IN

Makes 2 cups

1 cup mayonnaise
1 cup sour cream
1¹/₂ Tbsp. minced onion
1 Tbsp. chopped fresh parsley
1 tsp. chopped fresh dill
¹/₂ tsp. seasoned salt

¹/₄ tsp. garlic powder
³/₄ cup finely diced and
   seeded cucumber
   (optional)
dash of hot pepper sauce
   (optional)

1. Mix together mayonnaise and sour cream.
2. Add remaining ingredients. Mix well.
3. Cover and chill for several hours.
4. Serve with raw vegetables or crackers.

Garlic-Dill Dip

Gerry Janus
Vileniki—An Herb Farm
Montdale, PA

Makes 1 pint

1 cup sour cream
³/₄ cup plain yogurt
2 small cloves garlic, finely
   minced, or put through
   garlic press
1 Tbsp. minced fresh dill
   (1 tsp. dried)
4 Tbsp. minced fresh
   parsley (1¹/₂ tsp. dried)

2 Tbsp. minced fresh
   chives (2 tsp. dried)
¹/₂ tsp. finely minced fresh
   lovage
¹/₂ tsp. celery salt
dash of cayennne pepper

1. Blend together sour cream and yogurt.
2. Add garlic, herbs, and seasonings, and blend well.
3. Refrigerate for several hours to allow flavor to develop. Serve
   with raw vegetables, chips, or crackers.

Dill-Radish Dip

Kathleen Brown
Brown Horse Herb Farm
Lakewood, CO

Makes 2 cups

8-oz. pkg. cream cheese,
softened
1 Tbsp. lemon juice
3/4 tsp. chopped fresh
dill (1/4 tsp. dried)

1/2 - 3/4 tsp. salt
1 clove garlic, minced
1 cup chopped radishes

1. Mix together cream cheese, lemon juice, dill, salt, and garlic.
2. Stir in chopped radishes. Mix until blended. Cover. Refrigerate
for at least 2 hours before using.
3. Serve with crackers or fresh vegetables.

Herb Garden Dip
"No Salt, All Herbs"

Carol Vaughn
Healthy Horse Herb Farm
Onley, Va

Makes 12 servings

8-oz. pkg. cream cheese,
softened, or sour cream
2 Tbsp. fresh rosemary
(2 tsp. dried)
2 Tbsp. fresh sage
(2 tsp. dried)
2 Tbsp. fresh lovage
(2 tsp. dried)

2 Tbsp. fresh parsley
(2 tsp. dried)
2 Tbsp. fresh basil
(2 tsp. dried)
1 Tbsp. dried minced onion,
or 1 tsp. garlic powder

1. Chop herbs; then mix together all ingredients.
2. Chill for several hours before serving.
3. Serve with crackers or fresh vegetables.

Green Dip

Jacoba Baker & Reenie Baker Sandsted
Baker's Acres
Groton, NY

Makes 2 cups

3 cups Swiss chard leaves, packed
3/4 cup fresh basil leaves
3 cloves garlic
1/2 cup olive oil
1 cup feta cheese, crumbled

1/2 cup walnuts, coarsely chopped
3/4 cup whipping cream
1/4 cup minced green onion
freshly ground pepper to taste

1. In blender, mix together chard leaves, basil leaves, garlic, olive oil, feta cheese, and walnuts until a paste forms.
2. Stir in whipping cream, onions, and pepper.
3. Use as a dip for fresh vegetables.

Black Bean Dip

Eone Riales
Fogg Road Herb Farm
Nesbit, MS

Makes 2 1/2 cups

15-oz. can black beans, rinsed, drained
1/3 cup mayonnaise
1/2 cup sour cream
4-oz. can chopped green chilies, drained
2 Tbsp. chopped fresh cilantro

3 tsp. chili powder
1 1/2 tsp. hot pepper sauce of your choice
1 tsp. garlic powder
1 tsp. salt (optional)
1 Tbsp. cilantro

1. Mash beans with fork.
2. Stir in all remaining ingredients except 1 Tbsp. cilantro until well blended.
3. Refrigerate. Garnish with 1 Tbsp. cilantro and serve with tortilla chips.

Dill-Radish Dip

Kathleen Brown
Brown Horse Herb Farm
Lakewood, CO

Makes 2 cups

8-oz. pkg. cream cheese,
  softened
1 Tbsp. lemon juice
3/4 tsp. chopped fresh
  dill (1/4 tsp. dried)

1/2 - 3/4 tsp. salt
1 clove garlic, minced
1 cup chopped radishes

1. Mix together cream cheese, lemon juice, dill, salt, and garlic.
2. Stir in chopped radishes. Mix until blended. Cover. Refrigerate for at least 2 hours before using.
3. Serve with crackers or fresh vegetables.

Herb Garden Dip
"No Salt, All Herbs"

Carol Vaughn
Healthy Horse Herb Farm
Onley, Va

Makes 12 servings

8-oz. pkg. cream cheese,
  softened, or sour cream
2 Tbsp. fresh rosemary
  (2 tsp. dried)
2 Tbsp. fresh sage
  (2 tsp. dried)
2 Tbsp. fresh lovage
  (2 tsp. dried)

2 Tbsp. fresh parsley
  (2 tsp. dried)
2 Tbsp. fresh basil
  (2 tsp. dried)
1 Tbsp. dried minced onion,
  or 1 tsp. garlic powder

1. Chop herbs; then mix together all ingredients.
2. Chill for several hours before serving.
3. Serve with crackers or fresh vegetables.

Green Dip

Jacoba Baker & Reenie Baker Sandsted
Baker's Acres
Groton, NY

Makes 2 cups

3 cups Swiss chard leaves, packed
3/4 cup fresh basil leaves
3 cloves garlic
1/2 cup olive oil
1 cup feta cheese, crumbled

1/2 cup walnuts, coarsely chopped
3/4 cup whipping cream
1/4 cup minced green onion
freshly ground pepper to taste

1. In blender, mix together chard leaves, basil leaves, garlic, olive oil, feta cheese, and walnuts until a paste forms.
2. Stir in whipping cream, onions, and pepper.
3. Use as a dip for fresh vegetables.

Black Bean Dip

Eone Riales
Fogg Road Herb Farm
Nesbit, MS

Makes 2 1/2 cups

15-oz. can black beans, rinsed, drained
1/3 cup mayonnaise
1/2 cup sour cream
4-oz. can chopped green chilies, drained
2 Tbsp. chopped fresh cilantro

3 tsp. chili powder
1 1/2 tsp. hot pepper sauce of your choice
1 tsp. garlic powder
1 tsp. salt (optional)
1 Tbsp. cilantro

1. Mash beans with fork.
2. Stir in all remaining ingredients except 1 Tbsp. cilantro until well blended.
3. Refrigerate. Garnish with 1 Tbsp. cilantro and serve with tortilla chips.

12

Antipasto Cheese and Olives

Shari Jensen
Crestline Enterprises
Fountain, CO

Makes 6-8 servings

1/2 cup medium or
large pitted black olives
1/4 cup medium sharp cheddar
cheese, cut into strips to
stuff black olives
1/2 lb. mozzarella cheese,
cut in 1/2" cubes
1/2 red or green bell pepper,
cut in 3/4" pieces
1/2 cup stuffed green olives

1/2 cup white wine vinegar
1/3 cup olive oil
1/2 tsp. minced garlic
1 Tbsp. fresh oregano
(1 tsp. dried)
1 tsp. crushed red pepper
flakes
1 1/2 tsp. fresh thyme
(1/2 tsp. dried)

1. Stuff cheddar sticks into black olives.
2. Combine mozzarella cubes, bell pepper
   pieces, and black and green olives. Set
   aside.
3. In saucepan, combine vinegar, oil,
   garlic, oregano, red pepper, and
   thyme. Cook until heated, but not
   boiling. Pour over olive and cheese
   mixture. Cool to room temperature.
4. Marinate in refrigerator for 1-3 days.
   Let stand at room temperature for 30
   minutes before serving.
5. Drain and serve with mushrooms, sala-
   mi, and/or good bread.

Olive Spread

Marian E. Sebastiano
Salt Box Gallery Herbs
Hubbard, OH

Makes 8 servings

1 cup Greek olives,
  pits removed
2 cloves garlic
2 tsp. lemon juice
1 tsp. capers
1 tsp. Dijon mustard
2 tsp. fresh parsley
  (2/3 tsp. dried)

2 tsp. fresh thyme
  (2/3 tsp. dried)
3-4 Tbsp. olive oil
baguette, or toasted
  pita bread
4-6 Tbsp. butter
1/4 cup Parmesan cheese

1. In food processor, mix together olives, garlic, lemon juice, capers, mustard, parsley, and thyme. Process until mixed but not smooth.
2. Blend in olive oil to hold mixture together.
3. Cut baguette into 3/4" slices. Spread with butter and then with olive mixture. Sprinkle with Parmesan cheese. Toast under broiler until lightly browned.
4. Serve bread with additional Olive Spread.

Grilled Bread with Onions and Cheese

Arlene Shannon
Greenfield Herb Garden
Shipshewana, IN

Makes 2 servings

4 slices good Italian bread,
  cut 1/2" thick
flavored olive oil
1 red onion, sliced thin
1/4 cup chopped fresh
  thyme, oregano, or rosemary

1 tomato, sliced thin
4 thin slices Romano
  or Parmesan cheese

1. Broil bread until lightly browned.
2. Brush both sides of browned bread with olive oil.
3. Lightly saute onion slices in flavored oil until limp but not crispy. Drain onion.
4. Layer each piece of bread with onion, chopped herb, and tomato. Top with cheese.
5. Broil until cheese melts. Serve immediately.

Pesto Pizza Rounds

Kathleen Brown
Brown Horse Herb Farm
Lakewood, CO

Makes 15-20 servings

2 cups fresh basil
2 large garlic cloves
1/2 cup Parmesan cheese
1/4 cup pine nuts
1/2 cup olive oil

salt to taste
pepper to taste
2 baguettes, sliced 1/2" thick
1/2 cup pizza sauce
1/2 cup Parmesan cheese

1. To make pesto, blend together basil, garlic, 1/2 cup Parmesan cheese, and pine nuts in food processor or blender. Process until smooth. Slowly add olive oil. Add salt and pepper. Process until well blended.
2. Lay slices of bread on cookie sheet. Spread a little pizza sauce and a dollop of pesto on each slice of bread. Top with a sprinkle of the remaining 1/2 cup Parmesan.
3. Place under broiler about 3 minutes, or until cheese is bubbly and bread is toasted. Serve hot or at room temperature.

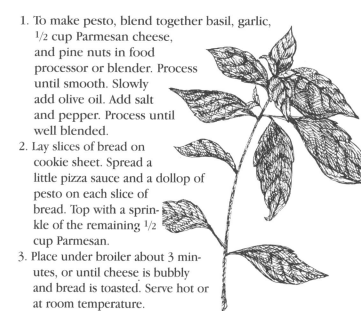

Herbal Garlic Bread

Lynn Redding
Redding's Country Cabin
Ronda, NC

Makes 10 servings

2 cloves garlic, minced
2 tsp. olive oil
2 Tbsp. chopped fresh parsley
 (2 tsp. dried)
2 Tbsp. chopped fresh thyme
 (2 tsp. dried)

$^1/_2$ tsp. paprika
2 Tbsp. grated Parmesan
 cheese
2 small loaves
 (4-oz. each) Italian
 or French bread

1. Combine garlic and oil. Mix well.
2. Combine parsley, thyme, and paprika. Stir in cheese. Mix well.
3. Angle your knife on the diagonal and slice bread into $^1/_2$ inch slices, without cutting all the way through bottom crust.
4. Brush cut sides of slices with garlic mixture. Sprinkle herb mixture between slices. Wrap bread in foil and place on baking sheet.
5. Bake at 350° for 10-15 minutes. Open the foil and place loaves under broiler for a minute or two to brown the tops. Serve immediately.

Herb Toastettes

Maryland Massey
Maryland's Herb Basket
Millington, MD

Makes 8 servings

$^1/_2$ cup butter or margarine,
 softened
2 Tbsp. sesame seeds
$^3/_4$ tsp. fresh marjoram
 ($^1/_4$ tsp. dried)
$^3/_4$ tsp. fresh basil
 ($^1/_4$ tsp. dried)

$^3/_4$ tsp. fresh rosemary
 ($^1/_4$ tsp. dried)
$^3/_4$ tsp. fresh chives
 ($^1/_4$ tsp. dried)
8-oz. loaf of party rye
 or other flavored bread

1. Mix together butter, sesame seeds, and chopped herbs.
2. Spread on bread slices. Place on cookie sheet.
3. Bake at 350° for 6-8 minutes, until slightly browned.

Herb Cheese Log

Toni Anderson
Cedarsbrook Herb Farm
Sequim, WA

Makes 10-12 servings

1 log Montrachet goat cheese
4 cloves garlic, minced
1/2 cup olive oil
2 large fresh or dried bay leaves,
  torn in several pieces
2 Tbsp. chopped fresh thyme
  (2 tsp. dried thyme)

2 Tbsp. butter, melted
1 Tbsp. olive oil
2 cloves garlic, minced
sourdough baguettes,
  sliced thin
fresh thyme

1. In mixing bowl combine 4 cloves
   garlic, 1/2 cup olive oil, bay
   leaves, and thyme.
2. Place cheese log in bread pan
   and baste well with oil mixture. Refrigerate for 24 hours,
   basting occasionally.
3. Mix together butter, 1 Tbsp.
   olive oil, and 2 cloves garlic.
4. Brush on sliced baquettes. Place
   on cookie sheet.
5. Bake at 325° for 15-20 minutes,
   until toasted.
6. To serve, place cheese log on
   serving dish. Remove bay
   leaves. Garnish with fresh
   thyme. Serve with baguettes.

Hot Herb Bread

Cassius L. Chapman
Mr. C's Cooking Castle
Tucker, GA

Makes 4 servings

1 loaf French bread
1/2 cup butter at room
 temperature
1 large clove garlic, minced
1/4 cup chopped fresh parsley
 (5 tsp. dried)

1 1/2 tsp. chopped fresh
 oregano (1/2 tsp. dried)
2 Tbsp. chopped fresh chives
 (2 tsp. dried)
salt to taste
pepper to taste

1. Cut bread into slices 1 1/2" thick, but do not cut the whole way through the loaf so the bread slices remain attached at the bottom.
2. Cream together butter and remaining ingredients. Spread mixture on each side of the slices. Wrap bread in foil, leaving top open.
3. Bake at 375° for 10 minutes. Serve hot.

Layered Cheese Torte with Pesto

Jacoba Baker & Reenie Baker Sandsted
Baker's Acres
Groton, NY

Makes 14-16 servings

Pesto Filling:
2 1/2 cups lightly packed
 fresh basil
1 cup freshly grated Parmesan
 or Romano cheese
1 lb. cream cheese, softened
1 lb. unsalted butter, softened

1/3 cup olive oil
1/4 cup pine nuts, chopped
salt to taste
pepper to taste
fresh basil sprigs

1. In blender or food processor, whirl basil leaves, Parmesan cheese, and olive oil until a paste forms. Stir in pine nuts, salt, and pepper. Set pesto aside.

18

2. Cream together cream cheese and butter until smoothly blended.
3. Cut 2 18" squares of cheesecloth or unbleached muslin. Moisten with water and ring dry. Use cloth to line a 5-6 cup loaf pan. Drape excess cloth over rim of mold.
4. Spread 1/6th of cheese mixture in prepared mold. Cover with 1/5th of pesto filling. Repeat until mold is filled, finishing with cheese.
5. Fold ends of cloth over top and press down lightly with hands to pack the mixture together..
6. Chill until firm, about 1-1 1/2 hours. (If the torte is allowed to stand longer in the pan, the cloth will act as a wick and cause the filling color to bleed onto the cheese.)
7. Invert onto serving dish and remove cloth. (The torte can be wrapped in plastic and refrigerated up to 5 days.)
8. Before serving, garnish with basil sprigs.
9. Spread on bread or vegetables.

Mango Salsa

Kelly Stelzer
Elderflower Farm
Roseburg, OR

Makes 8 servings

1 cup plum tomatoes, diced
1 cup mangoes, peeled and diced
1/4 cup sweet red or green bell peppers, diced
1 Tbsp. chopped fresh cilantro (1 tsp. dried), or 2 Tbsp. chopped fresh mint leaves, slightly mashed (2 tsp. dried)

1/4 cup chopped scallions
2/3 cup fresh lime juice (about 2 or 3 limes)
1/8 tsp. salt
1/8 tsp. pepper
1/2 tsp. zest of lemon or lime
1 fresh jalapeno pepper, seeded and minced

1. Mix together all ingredients. Stir well. Let stand at room temperature for 30 minutes.
2. Keeps in refrigerator for up to a week.
3. Serve with grilled chicken, fish, black beans and rice, or any jerked dish.

Variation: Mix salsa into 2 8-oz. packages of softened cream cheese and serve with crackers.

Fresh Tomato Salsa

Kathy Mathews
Heavenly Scent Herb Farm
Fenton, MI

Makes 2 cups

4 large plum tomatoes
1/4 cup chopped scallions
1/4 cup chopped fresh cilantro
1 Tbsp. chopped fresh oregano
  (1 tsp. dried)
2 cloves garlic, minced

1 tsp. minced jalapeno
  pepper, or to taste
1 Tbsp. olive oil
2 tsp. fresh lime juice
salt to taste
fresh black pepper to taste

1. Cut tomatoes in half lengthwise and remove the seeds. Cut halves into 1/4" pieces. Place in bowl.
2. Add remaining ingredients. Cover loosely and let stand at room temperature for 4 hours before serving.

Tomato-Basil Tart

Maryanne Schwartz and Tina Sams
The Herb Basket
Landisville, PA

Makes 8 appetizer servings
or 4 main dish servings

9" pie crust
1 1/2 cups shredded mozzarella
  cheese (6 oz.)
4 medium-sized tomatoes
1 cup loosely packed basil
  leaves (1/3 cup dried)

4 cloves garlic
1/2 cup mayonnaise
1/4 cup grated Parmesan
  cheese
1/8 tsp. ground white pepper
fresh basil leaves

1. Bake pie crust. Remove from oven. Sprinkle with 1/2 cup mozzarella. Cool on wire rack.
2. Dice tomatoes. Drain on paper towels. Arrange tomato chunks on melted cheese in baked pie shell.
3. Combine basil and garlic in food processor. Cover and process until chopped. Sprinkle over tomatoes.

4. Mix together remaining mozzarella, mayonnaise, Parmesan cheese, and pepper. Spoon cheese mixture over basil mixture, covering evenly.
5. Bake at 375° for 35 to 40 minutes, or until top is golden and bubbly. Garnish with fresh basil. Serve warm.

Guacamole

Barbara Sausser
Barb's Country Herbs
Riverside, CA

Makes 3 cups

2 medium-sized, very ripe
  avocados
1 small onion, grated fine
1 Tbsp. olive oil
dash of paprika
freshly ground pepper to taste
2 medium-sized ripe tomatoes,
  chopped

2 Tbsp. chili powder
2 tsp. lime juice
2 tsp. lemon juice
1 tsp. salt
1 tsp. ground coriander
1/2 cup shredded Jack cheese

1. Cut avocados in half, lengthwise. Remove pit or seed. Peel each half. Place in bowl and mash with a fork.
2. Stir in remaining ingredients, except cheese. Mix well.
3. Stir in cheese. Serve immediately.
4. Serve as a dip with tortilla chips, or as a condiment on enchiladas or tacos.

Mary's Mexican Munchies

Mary Peddie
The Herb Market
Washington, KY

Makes 8-10 servings

3 cups freshly shredded
   head lettuce
8-oz. pkg. cream cheese, softened
5 Tbsp. mayonnaise, milk,
   buttermilk, sour cream,
   or salsa juice
1 Tbsp. chopped fresh
   garlic chives
1/2 cup thinly sliced
   green onions
16-oz. can refried beans
few drops of oil
2 cloves garlic, minced
1 cup fresh tomatoes,
   finely chopped

1/2 cup chopped avocado
   (optional)
1/2 cup diced jicama,
   or cucumber
1 tsp. salt
16-oz. jar taco salsa,
   whatever strength you
   prefer
1 cup sour cream
1 cup shredded sharp
   cheddar cheese
3 Tbsp. chopped fresh
   cilantro
1/2 cup chopped black olives
corn chips or tortilla chips

1. Line a deep platter with a bed of freshly shredded head lettuce.
2. Mix together cream cheese, mayonnaise, or other liquid, and chives. Spread over lettuce.
3. Sprinkle onions over cream cheese mixture.
4. Mix together beans, oil, and garlic. Spread over onions.
5. Sprinkle tomatoes and avocado over beans.
6. Layer jicama or cucumbers over tomatoes and avocado. Salt lightly.
7. Pour salsa over jicama or cucumbers.
8. Top with a thin layer of sour cream. Cover with plastic wrap and chill for several hours before serving.
9. Before serving, garnish with cheese, cilantro, and black olives.
10. Serve with corn chips or tortilla chips.

Easy Swiss-Bacon Squares

Judy and Don Jensen
Fairlight Gardens
Auburn, WA

Makes 12-15 servings

8-oz. pkg. refrigerated
   crescent roll dough
8-10 slices bacon, fried,
   drained, crumbled
12-oz. shredded Swiss cheese

3 eggs, beaten
3/4 cup milk
1 Tbsp. minced chives
   (or any herb you wish)
1/2 tsp. salt

1. Press dough into a 9" x 13" pan.
2. Combine remaining ingredients and pour over dough.
3. Bake for 30 minutes at 375°. Remove from oven. Let stand for
   5 minutes, then cut into squares to serve.

Ham, Cream Cheese, and Chive Squares

Mary Ellen Warchol
Stockbridge Herbs & Stitches
South Deerfield, MA

Makes 8 servings

8-oz. pkg. cream cheese,
   softened
1/4 cup chopped fresh chives
   (5 tsp. dried)

8 slices imported ham
   (1/8" thick)

1. Mix together cream cheese and chives.
2. Spread 1-2 Tbsp. cheese mixture on slice of ham. Cover with
   another. Repeat until you have 4 slices of ham and 3 layers of
   cheese mixture. Make a second stack with remaining ham and
   cheese mixture.
3. Wrap in foil and place in freezer.
4. One hour before serving, remove from freezer. Defrost for half
   an hour. While still partially frozen, cut each into 16 squares.
   Place a toothpick through the center of each square. Place on
   serving dish and allow to defrost completely.

23

Dilled Green Beans

Marty Mertens & Clarence Roush
Woodstock Herbs
New Goshen, IN
Kathy Hertzler
Lancaster, PA

Makes 7 pints

4 lbs. fresh green beans,
   washed
1³/4 tsp. crushed red chile
   pepper
3¹/2 tsp. whole yellow
   mustard seed

7 heads fresh dill,
   or 3¹/2 tsp. dried dill seed
7 cloves garlic
5 cups vinegar
5 cups water
¹/2 cup salt

1. Cut beans into lengths to fit into pint jars.
   Pack beans into clean, hot jars.
2. To each jar add ¹/4 tsp. pepper, ¹/2 tsp.
   mustard seed, 1 head fresh dill, or ¹/3
   tsp. dill seed, and a garlic clove.
3. Combine vinegar, water, and salt. Heat
   to boiling.
4. Pour liquid over beans, leaving ¹/4"
   headspace. Seal and process in boiling water bath for 10 minutes.
5. Serve cold.

*Note: The beans' flavor improves
in time, so let sealed pints sit for several days before serving.*

Thyme-Mushroom Canapes

Carolee Snyder
Carolee's Herb Farm
Hartford City, IN

Makes 40 pieces, or about 10-12 servings

8-oz. pkg. cream cheese, softened	salt to taste
2 egg yolks	pepper to taste
1 small onion, grated	dash of Worcestershire sauce
4-oz. can mushrooms, drained, chopped	10 slices white bread
	2 Tbsp. chopped fresh thyme (2 tsp. dried)

1. Mix together cream cheese, egg yolks, onion, mushrooms, salt, pepper, and Worcestershire sauce. Stir well. Chill 30 minutes. Sir in half of thyme.
2. Cut crusts from bread. Cut each slice into 4 small squares. Place on cookie sheet. Broil until lightly toasted. Remove from oven and turn each square over.
3. Spread cheese mixture on each untoasted side, being careful to cover the bread completely, so there are no exposed edges to burn in the broiler. Sprinkle with remaining thyme.
4. Broil until bubbly.

Note: These can be made ahead and frozen. Follow directions, except do not broil after spreading cheese mixture on bread. To serve, defrost for 15-20 minutes, then broil and serve.

Herbs-Liscious Mushrooms

Carol Lacko-Beem
Herbs-Liscious
Marshalltown, IA

Makes 6 servings

1 large shallot,
  or 2 small ones, sliced
3 cloves garlic, cut in quarters
2 Tbsp. butter
16 oz. fresh mushrooms, whole
2 Tbsp. chopped fresh marjoram
  (2 tsp. dried)
1 Tbsp. chopped fresh oregano
  (1 tsp. dried)
1 1/2 tsp. chopped fresh
  basil (1/2 tsp. dried)
1 1/2 tsp. chopped fresh
  thyme (1/2 tsp. dried)
3/4 tsp. chopped fresh
  summer savory
  (1/4 tsp. dried)
1/4 cup dry red wine

1. Saute shallots and garlic in butter until tender. Add mushrooms. Stir and cook until tender and beginning to darken.
2. Add herbs and wine. Stir well. Continue to cook for 3-4 minutes. Serve immediately.

Salmon-Stuffed Mushrooms

Kathy Little Star
Indian River Herb Co.
Millsboro, DE

Makes 20 pieces

20 large, fresh, button
  mushrooms
1 Tbsp. hazelnut oil
1/4 cup chopped wild onions
2 Tbsp. chopped hazelnuts,
  walnuts, or pecans
1/4 tsp. chopped fresh dill
1/2 tsp. Worcestershire sauce
1/4 tsp. sea salt
4-oz. smoked or steamed
  salmon
salmon roe (optional)
minced, fresh, flat-leaf
  parsley (optional)

1. Clean mushrooms and remove stems. Place stem-side up in glass pie pan. Cover with foil.
2. Bake at 350° for 10 minutes, or until mushrooms are almost

tender. Turn mushrooms over onto paper towels to drain.
3. Stir together oil, onions, nuts, dill, Worcestershire sauce, and salt. Stir in salmon. Let sit for 20 minutes.
4. Fill mushroom caps with salmon mixture. Return to glass pie plate.
5. Bake at 350° for 3-5 minutes, or until salmon mixture is bubbly.
6. Garnish with salmon roe and minced parsley. Serve immediately.

Quick Salmon Mousse

Mary "Auntie M" Embler
Auntie M's Enchanted Garden
Clayton, NC

Makes 10 appetizer servings
or 4 salad servings

7 3/4-oz. can red salmon
3-oz. pkg. cream cheese, softened
2 Tbsp. lemon juice
6 drops Tabasco sauce

1/4 tsp. dry mustard
1/4 tsp. curry powder
1 tsp. chopped fresh dill
(1/3 tsp. dried)

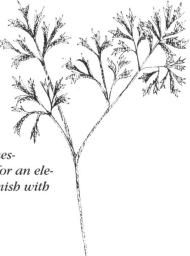

1. Drain salmon. Remove any bones or skin.
2. Combine all ingredients. Mix well and chill for 8 hours.
3. Serve with crackers.

Note: This mousse may be molded into any shape and nestled on a bed of fresh greens for an elegant salad presentation. Garnish with fresh parsley and dill.

Crabmeat Nibblers

Elaine Seibel
Scents and Non-Scents
Hill, NH

Makes 12 servings

12 oz. crabmeat, cleaned	6 English muffins,
1 cup grated cheddar cheese	split in half
1/4 cup mayonnaise	paprika
1 tsp. prepared mustard	
1 Tbsp. fresh dill (1 tsp. dried)	

1. Combine crabmeat, cheese, mayonnaise, mustard, and dill. Mix until well blended.
2. Spread on English muffins. Place on baking sheet and sprinkle with paprika.
3. Broil 5" from heat for 2-5 minutes, or until golden brown and bubbly. Cut into quarters. Serve warm.

Karozott

Shatoiya de la Tour
Dry Creek Herb Farm
Auburn, CA

Makes 3 cups

2 8-oz. pkgs. cream cheese,	2 tsp. anchovy paste
softened	1 cup chopped fresh chives
1/4 cup butter, softened	(1/3 cup dried)
1/2 lb. blue cheese, softened	2 tsp. paprika
1/2 tsp. caraway seeds, or	
11/2 tsp. chopped,	
fresh caraway thyme	

1. Mix together cream cheese, butter, and blue cheese. Blend well.
2. Stir in caraway seeds or thyme, anchovy paste, chives, and paprika.
3. Serve with crackers or stuffed in celery or olives.

Note: Karozott is a traditional Hungarian cheese dip— rich, but loved!

Rosemary Cheese Twists

Gerry Janus
Vileniki—An Herb Farm
Montdale, PA

Makes about 5 dozen twists

1 cup unbleached flour
1/4 tsp. cayenne pepper
2 Tbsp. chopped fresh
   rosemary (4 tsp. dried)
1/4 cup cold butter,
   cut into chunks

1/2 cup shredded sharp
   cheddar cheese
1 egg yolk
ice water

1. Mix together flour, cayenne pepper, and rosemary. Cut in butter until mixture is crumbly.
2. Stir in cheese and egg yolk. Mix well. Add ice water a teaspoon at a time until a stiff dough is formed.
3. Roll dough to 1/4" thickness between two sheets of wax paper. Cut into strips 3" x 1/2". Twist strips several times and place on greased baking sheet.
4. Bake at 400° for 9 minutes, or until lightly browned. Cool on rack. Store in tightly covered tin.

Pecans Rosemary

Mary Ellen Warchol
Stockbridge Herbs & Stitches
South Deerfield, MA

Makes 8-12 servings

2 Tbsp. melted butter
1/8 tsp cayenne pepper
1 1/2 Tbsp. finely chopped
  fresh rosemary (1 1/2 tsp. dried)

2 cups pecan halves
salt to taste

1. Mix together butter, pepper, and rosemary. Add pecans and toss well.
2. Spread pecans in baking pan.
3. Bake at 350° for 8-10 minutes, stirring once or twice while baking. Cool.
4. Sprinkle with salt if desired.

Rosemary House Walnuts

Bertha Reppert
The Rosemary House
Mechanicsburg, PA

Makes 2 cups

4 Tbsp. butter or margarine,
  melted
4 Tbsp. finely chopped fresh
  rosemary (4 tsp. dried)

1/2 tsp. salt (optional)
1 tsp. paprika
1 lb. walnut halves

1. Mix together butter and seasonings in shallow baking pan. Stir in nuts. Mix until well coated.
2. Bake at 350° for 8 minutes. Nuts crisp as they cool.

Variation: Substitute cayenne pepper for paprika.

Spicy Peanut Dip

Kathleen Brown
Brown Horse Herb Farm
Lakewood, CO

Makes 1 cup

1/2 cup smooth peanut butter
1/4 cup minced onion
1/4 cup fresh lemon juice
1 Tbsp. soy sauce

2 cloves garlic, minced
1 tsp. ground coriander
1/4 cup chopped fresh
    parsley (5 tsp. dried)

1. Mix together all ingredients in blender for 1 minute.
2. Serve at room temperature. Use as dip for veggies or crackers.

Basiled Cracker Bites

Jacoba Baker & Reenie Baker Sandsted
Baker's Acres
Groton, NY

Makes 6-8 servings

10 oz. oyster crackers
1/3 cup salad oil
1 pkg. Hidden Valley
    Ranch House seasoning

3 Tbsp. chopped fresh basil
    (1 tsp. dried)
1 large clove garlic

1. Pour crackers into large microwave-safe bowl.
2. Blend remaining ingredients in blender until smooth. Pour over crackers. Mix well.
3. Microwave on High for 2 minutes. Cool and serve.

Note: These will keep for several weeks in an airtight container.

Herbed Party Mix

Dawn Ranck
Harrisonburg, VA

Makes 8 cups

2 cups wheat chex cereal
2 cups corn chex cereal
2 cups rice chex cereal
3/4 cup nuts
1 cup little pretzels
   chives
8 Tbsp. butter, melted

4 tsp. Worcestershire sauce
1 tsp. seasoned salt
2 tsp. dried thyme
3 tsp. dried dill
4 tsp. dried

1. In large bowl, mix together cereal, nuts, and pretzels. Set aside.
2. Mix together butter, Worcestershire sauce, seasoned salt, thyme, dill, and chives. Pour over cereal and mix until well coated.
3. Bake at 250° for 1 hour, stirring every 15 minutes. Cool before serving or storing.

About the Authors

Dawn J. Ranck is an advocate of bringing herbs to everyone's kitchens, not just to the cooking artists'.

A resident of Harrisonburg, Virginia, she is also the co-author of *A Quilter's Christmas Cookbook*.

Phyllis Pellman Good, Lancaster, Pennsylvania, has had her hand in many cookbooks—among them, *The Best of Amish Cooking, Recipes from Central Market,* and *The Best of Mennonite Fellowship Meals.*